Reviews for SENIOR TRIVIA from trivia experts and addicts:

"I thoroughly enjoyed SENIOR TRIVIA. As a long-time television viewer and avid movie fan, this book brought back many memories and gave me hours of fun...."

—*Allen Blackmon, Elkhart, IN*

"As a kid, I probably watched as much television and movies as anyone. Some of these questions even stumped me, but they were so much fun!"....

—*Nancy Blundy, Jacksonville, IL*

"SENIOR TRIVIA was a perfect gift for me! It really brought back the good old days. How often do you get reminded of the comic books your read as a kid, and especially the radio programs we listened to, just before the onslaught of television?" ...

—*Diane Rogers, Dunedin, FL*

Senior Trivia

Senior Trivia

Fun Trivia Questions from the Golden Age of Entertainment

D. L. King

iUniverse, Inc.

New York Lincoln Shanghai

Senior Trivia
Fun Trivia Questions from the Golden Age of Entertainment

Copyright © 2008 by Dick L. King

iUniverse books may be ordered through booksellers or by contacting:

iUniverse
2021 Pine Lake Road, Suite 100
Lincoln, NE 68512
www.iuniverse.com
1-800-Authors (1-800-288-4677)

Because of the dynamic nature of the Internet, any Web addresses or links contained in this book may have changed since publication and may no longer be valid.

The views expressed in this work are solely those of the author and do not necessarily reflect the views of the publisher, and the publisher hereby disclaims any responsibility for them.

ISBN: 978-0-595-48108-8 (pbk)
ISBN: 978-0-595-60206-3 (ebk)

Printed in the United States of America

Contents

SENIOR TRIVIA

Test Your Memory with Fun Trivia Questions from the Golden Age of Entertainment!

Baby Boomers and Seniors will Enjoy answering questions from 1950's and '60's Television, Radio, Motion Pictures, and Comic Books.

Who was the host of the CBS quiz show "G. E. College Bowl?" What actress did he marry?

What comic book superhero who had a magic green ray-ring?

What comic radio personalities had a disaster each time they opened their closet?

Who starred as the narrator in the first "Godzilla" movie?

Gather some friends and share the memories. This book is a compilation of fun questions on entertainment from the 1950's and '60's. The baby boomers of today who were born near the end of World War II will remember listening to radio, near the end of the radio era, and watching television near the beginning of its Golden Age. In addition, this book features questions from classic movies and comic books you read as a youngster.

So, who was the host of "G. E. College Bowl?" Did you guess Allen Ludden? The contestants were three teams of players from various colleges and universities. Each question, depending on the difficulty, was assigned a set amount of points. Mr. Ludden would announce a "toss-up" question whereby the contestants could hit their buzzers to try for a correct answer. If they were wrong, they were penalized, and the question was open for others to try. If answered correctly, the toss-up question was followed by bonus questions for additional points. By the way, Allen Ludden married Betty White, who starred in television and motion pictures. She was best known for her later role in "The Golden Girls."

The comic book character with the magic ring? Of course, he was "Green Lantern."

The comic radio duo with the crowded closet was "Fibber McGee and Molly."

The narrator from the original "Godzilla" movie was Raymond Burr.

Enjoy the questions! The answers start on page 79.

TELEVISION

Game Shows

1. Who was the host of "Masquerade Party?"

2. Name the host of "Play Your Hunch."

3. Who was Groucho Marx's announcer on "You Bet Your Life?"

4. Herb Shriner hosted this game show. It was sponsored by Old Gold Cigarettes and featured the Old Gold Dancers, leggy girls dressed in Old Gold Cigarette packs.

5. Name two of the longest-running panel members from "To Tell the Truth? Who was the host of the show?

6. Name two of the first three hosts of "Name That Tune."

7. Name the singer on "Name That Tune" from the '70's. She later became the co-host of a popular morning talk show.

8. Name one of the two hosts of "$64,000 Challenge."

9. Who was the host of "Dollar a Second?"

10. Name the original host of "The Price is Right."

11. Who was the host of "Beat the Clock?"

12. Who was the blonde female assistant on "Beat the Clock?"

13. Name the host of "Dotto."

14. Name the host of "Tic Tac Dough."

15. Name the host of "Strike It Rich."

16. Who was the original host of "What's My Line?"

17. Name the three longest-running panel members of "What's My Line?"

18. What was the famous "What's My Line?" question asked about the size of an object?

19. Name the original host of "I've Got a Secret."

20. Winston Cigarettes sponsored "I've Got a Secret." What was Winston's slogan?

21. Name three of the longest-running panel members of "I've Got a Secret."

22. Name three of the panel members from "Stump the Stars."

23. Who hosted the "$64,000 Question?"

24. Name the host of "Dough Re Mi."

25. Name the host of "Queen for a Day."

26. Name two of the first three hosts of "Who Do You Trust?"

27. Who was the host of "Amateur Hour?"

28. Who hosted "The Match Game?"

Westerns

29. Who was the boy master of "Rin Tin Tin?"

30. What did Rin Tin Tin's master yell to get the dog to attack?

31. Name the U.S. Army Fort in "Rin Tin Tin."

32. Who played Jingles on "Wild Bill Hickock?"

33. Who played Wild Bill?

34. Name the star of "The Rebel."

35. Name the star (Paladin) of "Have Gun, Will Travel."

36. In what city did Paladin live?

37. Name Paladin's Chinese valet.

38. Name the star of "Wanted Dead or Alive."

39. What famous cowboy was portrayed by actor Leonard Slye?

40. Name Roy Rogers' theme song.

41. Who was Roy's sidekick on television?

42. Name the sidekick's jeep.

43. What was the sidekick's favorite exclamation?

44. Name Roy Rogers' dog.

45. What was the home town in the Roy Rogers television show?

46. Who portrayed "Hopalong Cassidy?"

47. Who was Hoppy's sidekick?

48. What was Gene Autry's theme song?

49. Who was Gene's sidekick on his television program?

50. What was the best-selling Christmas record sung by Gene Autry?

51. Who portrayed the Oxford-educated Indian on "Daniel Boone?"

52. Who was the lead actress of "Big Valley?"

53. Name the host of "Zane Grey Theater."

54. Name the Cisco Kid's sidekick.

55. Who played the father in "Fury?"

56. Name the star of "Coronado Nine," brought to you by Falstaff Beer?

57. What was the name of Annie Oakley's brother?

58. Name the star of "Yancy Derringer."

59. What was Yancy's sidekick's name, an Indian with a shotgun?

60. What role did Eric Fleming play on "Rawhide?" What tragic event happened to Mr. Fleming after "Rawhide?"

61. What role did Clint Eastwood play on "Rawhide?" What was the cook's name?

62. What popular characters did Clayton Moore and Jay Silverheels portray?

63. Who was the stiff-legged sidekick of Matt Dillon on "Gunsmoke?"

64. Who played Doc on "Gunsmoke?"

65. Who played Miss Kitty?

66. Who played the "half-breed" Quint for several shows on "Gunsmoke?"

67. Name the ranch on "Bonanza."

68. MATCHING

Match the western star with his/her horse:

_____1. Roy Rogers   A. Cocoa

_____2. Gene Autry   B. Topper

_____3. Dale Evans   C. Buttermilk

_____4. Rex Allen   D. Diablo

_____5. Cisco Kid   E. Champion

_____6. Hopalong Cassidy   F. Trigger

_____7. Lone Ranger   G. Scout

_____8. Tonto   H. Silver

Comedy Shows

69. Name Ozzie and Harriet's neighbor.

70. Name the star of "My Friend Irma."

71. Who was the star (Lilly Ruskin) of "December Bride?"

72. Who played the neighbor, Pete, in "December Bride?" He later starred in a spin-off, "Pete and Gladys" and later appeared in the t.v. hit "MASH."

73. What show featured a woman with young daughters, a train station, and Uncle Joe?

74. Who played the role of Cosmo in "Topper?" He later played a role in "Man from UNCLE."

75. Name the two human ghosts in "Topper."

76. Name the dog in "Topper."

77. Name the "George Burns and Gracie Allen" theme song.

78. Who was George Burns' announcer?

79. What did George Burns almost always have with him, his trademark?

80. What was the name of the show George Burns produced and starred in, after Gracie died?

81. Name the four stars of "I Love Lucy."

82. Who was the owner of "Mr. Ed?"

83. Who was Jack Benny's butler?

84. Who was Jack Benny's announcer?

85. Name Jack's singer-nemesis.

86. Who starred as the house detective on the "Jose Jimenez Show?" He later starred in a popular spin-off comedy spy show.

87. Who played Jose Jimenez?

88. Bob Crane was the star of "Hogan's Heroes." Who portrayed the English prisoner?

89. What game show did the English prisoner later host?

90. What character on "Hogan's Heroes" was portrayed by Werner Klemper?

91. Who starred in "I Married Joan?"

92. Name Dobie's best friend in "Dobie Gillis."

93. What did Herbert T. Gillis, Dobie's father, do for a living?

94. What actress played Dobie's girlfriend, Thailia Meninger?

95. What type character was Zelda, and what type was Chatsworth Osborne, Jr. on "Dobie Gillis?"

96. Name the star of "Sea Hunt."

97. Name the star of "Our Miss Brooks."

98. Who played Miss Brooks' principal?

99. Who portrayed Dexter, Miss Brooks' squeaky-voiced student?

100. Who was the star of "My Little Margie?"

101. Who was Margie's dad's boss?

102. Where did Gale Storm's "Oh! Susanna" take place?

103. Who was the star of the Army comedy "You'll Never Get Rich?"

104. What character did the star play on "You'll Never Get Rich?"

105. Who was the stupid private on "You'll Never Get Rich?"

106. Who played Bub on "My Three Sons?"

107. Name the creator of "Candid Camera."

108. Who starred in "Private Secretary?"

109. Name Milton Berle's 1948–1956 television show.

110. Name Milton Berle's t.v. secretary.

111. Name ventriloquist Jimmy Nelson's dummy.

112. Name five of the cast members from "Your Show of Shows."

113. Who starred as Beaver in "Leave it to Beaver?"

114. Who played the girl in "Peck's Bad Girl?"

115. Name the star of "Mr. Peepers."

116. Who played Mr. Peepers' know-it-all colleague, Harvey Weskit?

117. Who was the star of "Hennessey?"

118. Who played Hennessey's girl friend?

119. Name the two male leads in "The Real McCoys."

120. Who starred in "That's My Boy?"

121. Who starred in "Life with Riley?"

122. Who was Riley's wife?

123. What characters were Junior and Babbs on "Life with Riley?"

124. What character was Gillis on "Life with Riley?"

125. What did Riley say when things did not turn out the way he had planned?

126. Name the four main characters of Jackie Gleason's "The Honey-mooners."

127. What dancers performed on "The Jackie Gleason Show?" The camera shots included an overhead view of the dance performance.

128. Name the "TW3 girl" from "That Was the Week That Was."

129. Name Art Linkletter's two longest-running shows.

130. Name three of the five characters of "Mama."

131. Who was the main character on "Life with Father?"

132. Name the original title of Danny Thomas' show.

133. Who played Danny Thomas' wife?

134. Name the star of "Father Knows Best."

135. Name the three children of "Father Knows Best."

136. Who played Mr. Anderson's wife, Margaret, on "Father Knows Best?"

137. In what city did "Father Knows Best" take place?

138. Name five of the characters portrayed on t.v. by Red Skelton.

139. Who was George Gobel's wife?

140. Name George Gobel's band leader.

141. Name the two sisters from "Those Whiting Girls."

142. Who starred in "Meet Millie?"

143. Who played Gomer Pyle on the "Andy Griffith Show?"

144. What show did Gomer have as a spin-off, after he left Mayberry?

145. Who played Captain Parmeter on "F-Troop?"

146. Who played the scheming sergeant on "F-Troop?"

147. Who played the corporal on "F-Troop?"

148. Who played Herman on "The Munsters?"

149. Who played Lilly on "The Munsters?"

150. Who played McHale in "McHale's Navy?"

151. Name the captain in "McHale's Navy."

152. What comedy duo hosted "Laugh In?"

153. Name the actors who portrayed the dirty old man and prudish old lady on the park bench, on "Laugh In."

154. What CBS show copied "Laugh In," but as a country, hillbilly show?

155. Adam West and Burt Ward starred as Batman and Robin on "Batman." Name the actors who portrayed the following: Joker; Penguin; Riddler; Catwoman.

156. Name the popular show that starred Rob Reiner and Sally Strothers as a young married couple, living with her parents.

157. In "Car 54 Where Are You?," what police officers were portrayed by Ed Gwynne and Joe E. Ross?

158. On the "Smothers Brothers Show," what comedian ran for political office?

159. What show was the first spin-off of "All in the Family?"

160. Name the song sung by Carroll O' Connor and Jean Stapleton at the beginning of each episode of "All in the Family."

Children's Shows

161. Who played Timmy on "Lassie?"

162. Whom did George Cleveland portray on the original "Lassie?"

163. Name the two boys on the original "Lassie."

164. What space hero was played by Al Hodge?

165. What cartoon featured the adventures of a sea serpent and his pal?

166. Who was the hostess of "Ding Dong School?"

167. Name the female band leader of "Super Circus."

168. Who played "Captain Gallant" of the Foreign Legion?

169. What character was Fuzzy on "Captain Gallant?"

170. What character was Skipper on "Captain Gallant?"

171. Who played "Jungle Jim?" What famous character did he portray in the movies?

172. What character was Cuffy on "Jungle Jim?"

173. What was the name of Jungle Jim's chimp?

174. Name the show about a medical doctor in the jungle of India.

175. Who was the space hero who wore a black mask?

176. Who starred as "Robin Hood?"

177. Who was the host of "Howdy Doody?"

178. Who was the grouchy puppet on "Howdy Doody?"

179. Name the clown on "Howdy Doody."

180. On "Smilin' Ed's Gang" (also known as "Uncle Andy's Gang"), what did Midnight the Cat say?

181. On "Smilin' Ed's Gang" which animal "plucked his magic twanger?"

182. What character did Bob Keeshan portray on television?

183. Who was Bob Keeshan's sidekick?

184. Name the two main puppets on Keeshan's show.

185. Who was the cartoon character on Keeshan's show who could change himself into any object he chose?

186. Who were this cartoon character's arch-enemies, and who was his "wonder dog?"

187. Name the two mad magpie cartoon characters.

188. Who was the cartoon character with a big star on his head? (Viewers used a magic sheet placed on the t.v. screen to help him out of predicaments)

189. What town did "Mighty Mouse" defend?

190. Who was the cat villain in "Mighty Mouse?"

191. What was the title of Fran Allison's children's show?

192. What actor was Corky in "Circus Boy?" He later starred in a popular singing group.

193. Name the "Big Top" ringmaster.

194. What was the first line of "Pinky Lee's" song?

195. Who created "Alvin and the Chipmunks?"

Miscellaneous

196. Name three of the four longest-running singers in "Your Hit Parade."

197. What was the longest-running number one song on "Your Hit Parade?"

198. Name the lead sled dog from "Sergeant Preston of the Yukon."

199. What famous advertisement showed three tiny men dancing and singing in a sink basin?

200. Who starred as "Richard Diamond?" He was the son of which famous Hollywood movie star?

201. Name the actress who played Sam, the female radio operator on "Richard Diamond." Only her legs were shown on the show. She later became a famous t.v. star on her own.

202. Who starred as "Superman" in the original show?

203. Who appeared on "The Garry Moore Show" and later became a famous comedienne?

204. Who was the babbling, stuttering elderly lady on "The Garry Moore Show?"

205. Who was Garry Moore's announcer?

206. Name the co-star of "Mr. Lucky."

207. Name the two stars of "The Thin Man."

208. Name the dog on "The Thin Man."

209. Who was the blonde girl on "Hawaiian Eye?"

210. Name the words to the famous Phillip Morris ad.

211. Who starred in "Brave Eagle" and later as one of the "Aquanauts?"

212. Name the two stars of "Route 66."

213. What did "Loretta Young" call her character with the rolled-up braids?

214. Who hosted the "General Electric Theater?"

215. What was the original name of Ed Sullivan's variety show?

216. Name the host of "You Are There."

217. Who was the star of "Zorro?"

218. Name two of the three stars of "Checkmate."

219. Who starred in television's "The Greatest Show on Earth?"

220. Name one of the stars of "Soldiers of Fortune."

221. Who was the star of "Sea Hunt?"

222. What was the name of Buster Brown's dog who lived in a shoe?

223. Who hosted "Person to Person?"

224. Who hosted the Westinghouse Refrigerator ads?

225. Name the young female star of the "Tennessee Ernie Ford Show."

226. What was Ernie's favorite saying?

227. Who threw the hatchet at the wooden man cut-out on the famous clip from Johnny Carson's "Tonight Show?"

228. Name the original "Today Show" host.

229. Name the original "Tonight Show" host.

230. Name five of Steve Allen's famous "Tonight Show" guest regulars.

231. Who hosted the "Tonight Show" in 1957 and told the infamous "watercloset" joke?

232. Name Jack Paar's bandleader

233. Who was the orchestra leader of the "Perry Como Show?"

234. Who was fired on the air by Arthur Godfrey?

235. Name the star of "Coke Time."

236. What was the hit song Eddie Fisher's wife, Debbie Reynolds, sang on his show?

237. Name the television playhouse sponsored by Armstrong Tile.

238. What was the earliest television soap opera that was still running into the 1980's?

239. Whom did Rosemary Prinz play on "As the World Turns?"

240. Name the host of "Science Fiction Theater."

241. Who was "The Millionaire?"

242. Name the main character on "The Millionaire," the assistant who gave away the money.

243. What character did Barbara Hale play on "Perry Mason?"

244. Name Perry's private investigator.

245. Who was the star of "The Defenders?"

246. Who was "Ben Casey's" wise old doctor friend?

247. Who was "Dr. Kildare's" superior?

248. Who starred in "East Side, West Side?"

249. Name the star of "Public Defender."

250. Name the star of "Harbor Command."

251. Who played detective Frank Smith on "Dragnet?"

252. Name the stars of "Peter Gunn."

253. What famous man and wife were played by Barbara Britton and Richard Denning?

254. What was the name of the boat in James A. Michener's "Adventures in Paradise?"

255. Name "Sky King's" plane.

256. What character was Penney on "Sky King?"

257. What show concerned adventures and rescues with helicopters?

258. In what city did "The Lineup" take place?

259. Who played Eliot Ness in "The Untouchables?"

260. Who played Al Capone in "The Untouchables?"

261. Who hosted "The Big Story?"

262. What Boston detective was portrayed by Chester Morris?

263. Name the main character in "I Led Three Lives."

264. Name the three male stars of "77 Sunset Strip."

265. What hit song came from "77 Sunset Strip?"

266. Name the first anchor of "The CBS Evening News."

267. Name television's first news documentary series, starring Edward R. Murrow.

268. Who was the host of "Life Worth Living?"

269. Who were the two former major league players who hosted CBS' "Game of the Week?"

270. Name the star of "Manhunt."

271. Which city was "The Naked City?"

272. Name Robert Vaughn's and David McCallum's roles in "Man from UNCLE."

273. Name the two stars of "Girl from UNCLE."

274. Who starred in "The Courtship of Eddie's Father?"

275. Who starred in "Man with a Camera?"

276. Name the co-stars of "I Spy."

277. Name the two popular rock and roll shows (featuring the current hits) of 1965.

278. Who starred as "Honey West?"

279. Who were Johnny Carson's band leaders on the "Tonight Show?"

280. What was the first match-up for "Monday Night Football?"

281. Who was the star of "Wild Wild West?"

282. Who starred in "Hawaii Five-O?"

283. NBC showed the first prime time movie on television, called "Saturday Night at the Movies." Which movie debuted?

284. In what background did "Room 222" take place?

285. What show featured "Rate a Record" and "Spotlight Dance?"

286. What was Diahann Carroll's occupation in her show "Julia?"

287. Who played Donna Stone and on what show?

288. What popular NBC show first featured "Davy Crockett?"

289. Name the show in which Robert Young portrayed a doctor.

290. The first U.S. television interracial kiss was shared on an episode called "Plato's Stepchildren" of what popular series?

291. Who starred in "Voyage to the Bottom of the Sea?"

292. Who played the boy, Will Robinson, in "Lost in Space?"

293. Who played Granny in "The Beverly Hillbillies?"

294. Name the host and creator of "The Twilight Zone."

295. Name the ragtime piano and accordion player from "The Lawrence Welk Show."

296. Name the actors who portrayed the following characters of "Star Trek:"

    a. Captain James Kirk
    b. Mr. Spock
    c. Scottie
    d. Dr. "Bones" McCoy
    e. Sulu
    f. Chekov

297. MATCHING

Match the t.v. show with the sponsor.

_____1. Wild Bill Hickock   A. Lipton Tea

_____2. Gene Autrey   B. Sealtest

_____3. Lone Ranger   C. Carnation Milk

_____4. Amateur Hour   D. General Mills (Chee-rios)

_____5. Jack Benny (later years)   E. Good N Plenty

_____6. You Bet Your Life   F. Prudential

_____7. My Friend Irma   G. Kellogg's Corn Pops

_____8. George Burns & Gracie   H. State Farm Insurance
Allen

_____9. Ramar of the Jungle   I. Kool Cigarettes

_____10. Big Top   J. Mogen David Wine

_____11. Your Hit Parade   K. Geritol

_____12. You Are There   L. Doublemint Gum

_____13. Soldiers of Fortune   M. Seven-Up

_____14. Arthur Godfrey's Talent   N. Quick Home Perma-
Scouts   nent/Lucky Strike Ciga-rettes

_____15. Dollar A Second   O. Desoto

BONUS

TELEVISION COMMERCIALS

Match the commercial product with the quote:

a. "A little dab'll do ya. Simply rub a little in your hair."

b. "All my men are tigers. (woman lying on tiger skin) Grrrr."

c. "You like it. It likes you."

d. "Mabel, _____ _____!"

e. "It takes a licking and keeps on ticking!"

f. "What'll ya have? _____ _____ _____."

g. "Take it off. Take it all off!"

h. "Look sharp! Feel sharp!"

i. "Hits the spot!"

j. "Can't you keep Billy's bike out of the driveway!"

RADIO

298. Name the orchestra leader known as "The King of Jazz."

299. Who was the "First Lady of Radio" who reviewed plays in "Broadcasting Broadway?"

300. Name the Metropolitan Opera commentator.

301. Who played "the sweetest music this side of heaven?"

302. Who gave us such personalities as "Erno Rapee," "James Melton," and "Wee Willie Robyn?"

303. Who was the producer and star of "The Goldbergs?"

304. Who was known as "The Songbird of the South?"

305. Name the star of "The Breakfast Club."

306. Where did "The Breakfast Club" take place?

307. Name the show broadcasted by Norman Brokenshire and sponsored by Chesterfield Cigarettes.

308. Who starred on "Kraft Music Hall" along with Bob Burns and John Scott Trotter?

309. What female singer starred with Bing Crosby when he returned to radio in 1960?

310. Name the female singer who made these songs popular: "Love Me or Leave Me," "Ten Cents a Dance," and "Mean to Me."

311. On whose show did Bert Gordon appear as the "Mad Russian?"

312. Name the female singing trio of "National Barn Dance."

313. Who was the "Yowsah" man of "All the Lads?"

314. Name Joe Penner's famous catch phrase.

315. What was Major Bowes' signal that an amateur performer had failed on his "Amateur Hour?"

316. Name the show that began with machine guns, police sirens, and sounds from a prison yard?

317. Name the most popular star of broadcasting radio shows just for women.

318. Name the show that featured "Fanny" and "Father Barbour."

319. Name the show that began, "Wake up, America—time to stump the experts."

320. During World War II, who was the commentator famous for the phrase, "This … is London?"

321. Name the commentator with "the voice of doom."

322. Name the show that starred L. A. "Speed" Riggs as a tobacco auctioneer and Frank Sinatra as a singer.

323. What show created the $64.00 question?

324. Name the star of "Here's Morgan."

325. Name the famous mind reader of radio.

326. Name the show that had the "William Tell Overture" as its theme music.

327. Name as many of the famous radio mystery and suspense programs as you can.

328. Who was Phil Harris' wife and co-star?

329. Name the program that aired from the "Little Theater Off Times Square" and starred Olan Soule and Barbara Luddy.

330. Name the program introduced by Martin Horrell and frequently starring Neva Patterson.

331. Name the program starring Georgia Gibbs, Johnny Johnston, and Vera Ellen.

332. Name the show with characters such as: Senator Claghorn, Mrs. Nussbaum, Ajax Cassidy, and Titus Moody.

333. Who was the friend of Colonel Lemuel Q. Stoopnagle?

334. Name as many of the famous radio soap operas as you can.

335.   **MATCHING**

Match the radio stars to the show or character

_____1. "Perfect Fool"   A. Arthur Lake &
                                          Penny Singleton

_____2. "The Fleischman Hour"   B. Jim & Marian Jor-
                                          dan

_____3. "Town Hall Tonight"   C. Ed Gardner

_____4. "Baby Snooks"   D. Rudy Vallee

_____5. "Fibber McGee & Molly"   E. Roy Acuff & Bill
                                          Monroe

_____ 6. "The Aldrich Family"   F. Chet Lauck &
                                          Norris Goff

_____ 7. "Grand Ole Opry"   G. Fred Allen

_____8. "Duffy's Tavern"   H. Ezra Stone

_____9. "Life with Luigi"   I. Ed Wynn

_____10. "Alka Seltzer Time"   J. Fanny Brice

_____11. "Quiz Kids"   K. Herb Shriner

_____12. "Let's Pretend"   L. Nila Mack

_____13. "Lum and Abner"   M. Jan Murray

_____14. "Songs for Sale"   N. Clifton Fadiman

_____15. "Blondie and Dagwood"   O. J. Carrol Naish

COMIC BOOKS

336. Who was "Superman's" boss at the Daily Planet?

337. What did his boss exclaim whenever he was upset?

338. When "Mary Jane" said her magic words of "poof, poof, piffles," whom did she become as small as?

339. Who was the creator of "Tarzan?"

340. Name the serial that appeared in "Tarzan" comics that featured one white man and one black man.

341.Superman lived in Metropolis. Where did "Superboy" live?

342. Name the girl who was always pursuing Superboy, similar to Lois Lane pursuing Superman.

343. Name Superboy's dog.

344. Name the following relatives and characters of "Donald Duck."
    a. Three nephews
    b. Cheap-skate uncle
    c. Girlfriend
    d. Lucky cousin
    e. Inventor
    f. German professor
    g. Owner of the farm

345. Name the town where Donald Duck lived.

346. Name the three dog-faced criminals from "Donald Duck."

347. Name "Woody Woodpecker's" niece and nephew.

348. What magic word did "Captain Marvel" say to transform himself into the superhero?

349. What superhero got his red hero's uniform from a secret compartment in his ring?

350. Who was "Little Lu Lu's" fat friend?

351. Name the Little Lu Lu character with short, sparsely-grown hairs on his head.

352. Who was the little boy from "Little Lu Lu" to whom she told Witch Hazel stories?

353. Name the little girl who loved dots and always wore them on her dresses.

354. Who was the fat little girl who loved to eat?

355. Who was "Batman's" aunt?

356. Batman's secret identity was Bruce Wayne. What was Robin's?

357. Who was the underwater superhero who wore an orange shirt?

358. Which "Popeye" character ate a lot of hamburgers?

359. Who was "Porky Pig's" girlfriend?

360. Who was Porky's nephew?

361. Name the western hero with a whip.

362. Who was the female superhero with a transparent airplane?

363. What comic book featured the "Silent Knight" and the "Viking?"

364. What comic featured a fox and a crow?

365. Name "Henry Hawk's" sidekick.

366. Name "Mickey Mouse's" worst nemesis.

367. Name Mickey's nephews.

368. Name Minnie Mouse's nieces.

369. Who was the big, fat baby duck who had his own comic book?

370. Who was the little red-hot devil character?

371. Name the little wolf who wanted to be good, despite his "pop's" attitude.

372. What was "Zorro's" secret identity?

373. Who was Zorro's servant, and what disability did he have?

374. Name the fat sergeant who Zorro always out-smarted.

375. Name "Clarabelle Cow's" boyfriend.

376. Name the two playful chipmunks who always got into trouble.

377. Name the blonde, good-natured boxer in the comics.

378. Name the Indian who was referred to as the "Son of Stone."

379. Who was known as the "poor little rich boy?"

380. Who was the "good little witch?"

381. Name the following characters from "Archie" comics:

   a. Janitor
   b. Principal
   c. Cook
   d. Two girls fighting over Archie

382. Who was the little red-haired girl with the pony tail, who had her own comic book?

383. Who was "Red Ryder's" sidekick?

384. Who was "Green Arrow's" sidekick?

MOVIES

385. Who played the boxer in the re-make of "The Champ," originally starring Wallace Beery and Jackie Cooper?

386. Name the two main stars of "The Man Who Would Be King."

387. Claudette Colbert was the original "Cleopatra." Who starred in the re-make?

388. Name the two brothers who starred in "Trapeze."

389. Name the female star who played opposite Peter Sellers in "A Shot in the Dark."

390. In what movie did Peter Sellers first introduce his bumbling detective character?

391. Who played the main character in "Nevada Smith?" Who was the villain?

392. Who starred as a deaf mute in "The Heart is a Lonely Hunter?"

393. What lusty, earthy character was portrayed by Hugh Griffith in "Tom Jones?"

394. Who was the young wench portrayed by Diane Cilento in "Tom Jones?"

395. Who played opposite Albert Finney in "Tom Jones?"

396. Who played opposite Venessa Redgrave in "Blow-Up?"

397. What former NFL football star played in "1,000 Rifles?"

398. Name the actors/actresses who played the following roles in "Blazing Saddles:"

    a. San Francisco Kid
    b. Sheriff
    c. Lilly the dance hall girl
    d. Governor
    e. Land Baron
    f. Mongo

399. Who was the bad man who fought Alan Ladd in "Shane?"

400. Who played the boy, Joey Starrett, in "Shane?"

401. Name the three main stars of "The Apartment."

402. What company used the theme music to "The Apartment" for its commercials?

403. Name the four of the stars of "On the Waterfront."

404. Name the first James Bond film.

405. Who directed "Young Frankenstein?"

406. Name the actors/actresses who portrayed these roles in "Young Frankenstein:"

a. Dr. Frankenstein
b. The monster
c. The blind man
d. Dr. Frankenstein's girlfriend
e. The crazy old lady of Frankenstein's castle
f. Igor

407. What comedy duo starred in "Scared Stiff?" Where did it take place?

408. What was Clint Eastwood's occupation in "Play Misty for Me?"

409. What famous movie director portrayed the Cook County clerk at the end of the movie "Blues Brothers?"

410. Name the female actress who was abducted in the first re-make of "King Kong" after Fay Wray played the role?

411. Name the star of the "Incredible Shrinking Man."

412. Name the star of "Hercules" and "Hercules Unchained."

413. Name the two stars of "April Love."

414. What husband-wife team starred in "Forever Darling?"

415. Name the three stars of "The Good, the Bad, and the Ugly."

416. Name the professor of the "Dracula" movies.

417. Name the Wolfman's human name (originally played by Lon Chaney, Jr.).

418. Who played the evil mother in the original "Manchurian Candidate?"

419. Who directed "Exodus?"

420. Who played the lead role of Ari in "Exodus?"

421. Who played "Elmer Gantry?"

422. Name the two actors who portrayed slave friends in "Spartacus."

423. Name the two horror movie stars of "The Raven."

424. Who portrayed Franklin and Eleanor Roosevelt in "Sunrise at Campobello?"

425. Who starred as "El Cid?"

426. In what movie did Nancy Kwan play the lead role?

427. Name the two "Biblical actor" stars of "The Egyptian."

428. Who was the voice of the bear in "The Jungle Book?"

429. Name the movie about anti-Semitism that starred Gregory Peck, John Garfield, Celeste Holm, and Dorothy McGuire.

430. Name as many stars as you can of "All About Eve."

431. Who played the lead roles in "An American in Paris?"

432. Name these roles from "A Streetcar Named Desire:"
   a. Stanley
   b. Blanche
   c. Stella
   d. Blanche's suitor

433. Who played Shirley Booth's husband in "Come Back, Little Sheba?"

434. Name the later-famous actors who had these roles in horror movies:

    a. "The Blob"
    b. "I Was a Teenage Werewolf"
    c. Monster in the original "The Thing"

435. Who portrayed the circus owner in "The Greatest Show on Earth?"

436. Who was the clown in "The Greatest Show on Earth?"

437. Who was the trapeze artist in "The Greatest Show on Earth?"

438. Who was Maggio in "From Here to Eternity?"

439. Name the lead actor in "Stalag 17."

440. Name the actor who played the German spy in "Stalag 17."

441. Name the star of "The Barefoot Contessa."

442. Name the three main stars of "Country Girl."

443. Who played opposite Ernest Borgnine in "Marty?"

444. Who portrayed Ensign Pulver in "Mr. Roberts?" Who was the grouchy captain?

445. What was Ensign Pulver's last act in "Mr. Roberts?"

446. Who starred as himself in the autobiography "To Hell and Back?"

447. Who portrayed Phineas Fogg in "Around the World in 80 Days?"

448. Who played Eve White, Eve Black, and Jane, and in what movie?

449. Name the movie where a white man and black man were chained together as convicts. Who were the two stars?

450. Name the four stars of "Gigi."

451. Who played opposite David Niven in "Separate Tables?"

452. What role was played by Stephen Boyd in "Ben Hur?"

453. Name the star of "The Time Machine."

454. Who played Bernardo in "West Side Story?" Who played his girl-friend?

455. Who was opposite Paul Newman in "Hud?"

456. Name the three movies for which Katherine Hepburn won best actress Oscars.

457. What actress played opposite John Wayne in "The Quiet Man?"

458. Name John Wayne's character in "The Quiet Man."

459. Name John Wayne's character in "True Grit."

460. Who starred with Joseph Cotton in "Niagra?"

461. Name the song that came from Gary Cooper's movie "High Noon."

462. Who was the lead actor in "To Catch a Thief?" Who played opposite him?

463. Who played Emiliano Zapata in "Viva Zapata?" Who starred as his brother?

464. Name the star of "Lust for Life."

465. Name the four main stars of "The Bridge on the River Kwai."

466. Who starred in "Pollyanna?"

467. In what movie did Elizabeth Taylor star as Gloria Wandrous?

468. Name the bearded actor who frequently played supporting roles in John Wayne westerns.

469. Who played a sailor in "South Pacific" and later went on to star in "My Favorite Martian" on t.v.?

470. Name the two leads from "Mary Poppins."

471. Who played the father in "Mary Poppins?"

472. Name the three stars of "The Hustler."

473. Who starred with Peter O'Toole in "Lawrence of Arabia," portraying General Allenby?

474. Who was Gregory Peck's character in "To Kill a Mockingbird?"

475. Who portrayed Felix Unger and Oscar Madison in the movie "The Odd Couple?"

476. Name the star of "The Hanging Tree." Who was the villain?

477. This same actor portrayed a villain in which Marlon Brando western?

478. Name the two actresses who played opposite William Holden in "Picnic."

479. Name the two stars of "Love Me or Leave Me."

480. What actress, other than Elizabeth Taylor, appeared in the movie "Who's Afraid of Virginia Woolf?"

481. Who starred in "Fate is the Hunter?"

482. Who played Dr. Joyboy in "The Loved One?"

483. Who played Clyde's brother in "Bonnie and Clyde?"

484. What supporting actor portrayed a snotty-nosed character in the comedy "The Russians are Coming! The Russians are Coming!" and later appeared in "Bonnie and Clyde" as the one who set them up for the law to catch?

485. Who was the "Birdman of Alcatraz?"

486. Name the female star of "Cat Ballou."

487. Who won an Academy Award for his portrayal as a drunk cowboy in "Cat Ballou?"

488. Name the two singer-narrators of "Cat Ballou."

489. Name the star of "The Delicate Delinquent."

490. Which later-day comedy actor played the lead role in "Forbidden Planet?"

491. Name the lead actress in "I Want to Live."

492. Who played the crazed dental patient in the original "Little Shop of Horrors?"

493. Who portrayed Don Quixote in "Man of La Mancha?" Who played his sidekick?

494. Who played Arthur in "Camelot?"

495. Who played the queen in "Camelot?" Who was Lancelot?

496. Who played Colonel Pickering in "My Fair Lady?"

497. Who was Liza Doolittle in "My Fair Lady?" Whose voice was used for dubbing her songs?

498. In what body of water did you find the "Creature from the Black Lagoon?"

499. Name the three stars of "Singin' in the Rain."

500. Who starred as Jimmy Pearsall in "Fear Strikes Out?"

501. Who starred as Joe Hardy, opposite Gwen Verdon (Lola), in "Damn Yankees?

502. What actress appeared in "Valley of the Dolls" and was later a real-life murder victim in a famous case?

503. Name the movie starring Burt Lancaster, Montgomery Clift, Deborah Kerr, Frank Sinatra, and Donna Reed.

504. Who was Darby in "Darby O'Gill and the Little People?"

505. Who was the voice of "Frances the Talking Mule?" Who played his owner?

506. Name the actor who played the killer in Jimmy Stewart's "Rear Window."

507. Who was the star of "Blackboard Jungle?" What was the theme song?

508. Who played the disturbed captain from "The Caine Mutiny?"

509. Name the two stars of "Journey to the Center of the Earth."

510. Who was the sexy female star of "Fantastic Voyage?"

511. Name the campy movie about a distinguished alien who comes to earth to warn its inhabitants to stop warring.

512. Who played the lead in "Charly?"

513. Name the two stars of "Cactus Flower."

514. Who starred in "Born Yesterday?"

515. What movie starred Robert Culp, Eliott Gould, Dyan Canon, Natalie Wood, and Horst Ebersberg?

516. In what movie did Slim Pickens ride an atomic bomb like a horse?

517. Who played "Barabbas?"

518. Name the star of "Call Me Bwana."

519. Who was the "Wild One" who led a motorcycle gang?

520. In which movie did a shower of meteorites blind everyone who saw it, thus making them vulnerable to a terrifying horde of man-eating plants from outer space?

521. Who was the "Man with the X-Ray Eyes?"

522. Name the star of "Come Blow Your Horn."

523. What was Elvis Presley's first movie?

524. Who starred as "The Thoroughly Modern Millie?"

525. Name the director of "Rosemary's Baby."

526. Who played the Von Trapp family's father in "Sound of Music?"

527. The original "Cape Fear" starred Gregory Peck and Polly Bergan. Who was the villain?

528. Name the two stars of "Send Me No Flowers."

529. In what movie did Paul Newman win a contest by eating 50 hard-boiled eggs?

530. Name the "shocking" novel that was made into a movie starring James Mason, Sue Lyon, Shelley Winters, and Peter Sellers.

531. Name the star and villain of the original "House of Wax."

532. "Tora! Tora! Tora!" depicted what historical event?

533. Who portrayed Tarzan in "Tarzan and the Lost Safari?"

534. What famous song came from "Breakfast at Tiffanies?"

535. What famous comedy duo starred in 1952's "Jack and the Beanstalk?"

536. Name the star of "No Time for Sergeants." Who played the psychologist (he was later paired with the star in a popular t.v. series)?

537. Who starred as "Alfie?"

538. Who played Porgy in "Porgy and Bess?"

539. Name the three best-known stars of "Guess Who's Coming to Dinner?"

540. Name the popular movie in which Charlton Heston kneeled before the Statue of Liberty at the end.

541. What song-writing/singing pair did the musical score for "The Graduate?"

542. What was the hilarious one-word piece of advice Benjamin (Dustin Hoffman) received from Mr. McGuire, a family friend, at the graduation party in "The Graduate?"

543. In what western movie did Robert Redford and Paul Newman star as outlaws on the run?

544. Who played the small red-headed boy in "The Music Man?" Who played Professor Harold Hill?

545. Name who played Ned and who played Captain Nemo in "20,000 Leagues Under the Sea."

546. What was the name of the submarine in "20,000 Leagues Under the Sea?"

547. Who directed "The Ten Commandments?"

548. Name the country where "The King and I" took place.

549. This movie starred Yul Brynner and Steve McQueen as gunslingers who recruit five others and defend a Mexican village.

550. This movie is the same title as the popular Gene Pitney theme song. It starred John Wayne, James Stewart, and Lee Marvin.

ANSWER KEY

TELEVISION

Game Shows

1) Bud Collyer

2) Merv Griffin

3) George Fenneman

4) "Two for the Money"

5) Panel members were Tom Poston, Kitty Carlisle, Orson Beane, and host Bud Collyer

6) George de Witt, Bill Cullen, and Red Benson

7) Kathy Lee, later known as Kathy Lee Gifford and co-host of "Regis and Kathy Lee"

8) Sonny Fox, Ralph Story

9) Jan Murray

10) Bill Cullen

11) Bud Collyer

12) Roxanne

13) Jack Narz

14) Jack Barry

15) Warren Hull

16) John Daly

17) Bennet Cerf, Arlene Francis, Dorothy Kilgallen, Fred Allen (others were guest panelists after he died)

18) "Is it bigger than a breadbox?"

19) Garry Moore

20) "Winston tastes good like a cigarette should"

21) Bill Cullen, Henry Morgan, Betsy Palmer (or Jane Meadows), Faye Emerson (or Bess Myerson)

22) Diana Dors, Ross Martin, Sebastian Cabot, Beverly Garland

23) Hal March

24) Gene Rayburn

25) Jack Bailey

26) Edgar Bergan, Johnny Carson, Woody Woodbury

27) Ted Mack 28) Gene Rayburn

Westerns

29) Rusty

30) "Yo Ho, Rinty!"

31) Fort Apache

32) Andy Devine (Hey, Wild Bill, wait for me!")

33) Guy Madison 34) Nick Adams 35) Richard Booone 36) San Francisco

37) Heyboy

38) Steve McQueen

39) Roy Rogers

40) "Happy Trails to You"

41) Pat Brady

42) Nelly Bell

43) "Mustard and custard!"

44) Bullet

45) Mineral City

46) William Boyd

47) Lucky

48) "Back in the Saddle Again"

49) Pat Buttram

50) "Rudolph the Red—Nosed Reindeer"

51) Ed Ames

52) Barbara Stanwyck

53) Dick Powell

54) Pancho

55) Peter Graves (brother of James Arness)

56) Rod Cameron

57) Tagg

58) Jock Mahoney

59) Pahoo

60) Trail boss Gil Faver. Fleming later drowned in South America while shooting a movie

61) Rowdy Yates. The cook was "Wishbone" and the cook's assistant was "Mushy"

62) Lone Ranger and Tonto

63) Chester, portrayed by Dennis Weaver

64) Milburn Stone

65) Amanda Blake

66) Burt Reynolds

67) Ponderosa

68) MATCHING

Match the western star with his/her horse:

F	1. Roy Rogers	A. Cocoa
E	2. Gene Autry	B. Topper
C	3. Dale Evans	C. Buttermilk
A	4. Rex Allen	D. Diablo
D	5. Cisco Kid	E. Champion
B	6. Hopalong Cassidy	F. Trigger
H	7. Lone Ranger	G. Scout
G	8. Tonto	H. Silver

Comedy Shows

69) Thorny

70) Marie Wilson

71) Spring Byington

72) Harry Morgan, later played Colonel Potter on "MASH"

73) "Petticoat Junction"

74) Leo G. Carroll

75) George and Marian

76) Neil

77) "Just a Love Nest"

78) Harry Von Zell

79) cigar

80) "Wendy and Me"

81) Lucille Ball (Lucy), Desi Arnaz (Ricky), William Frawley (Fred), Vivian Vance (Ethel)

82) Wilbur Post (Alan Young)

83) Rochester (Eddie Anderson)

84) Don Wilson

85) Dennis Day

86) Don Adams, later the star of "Get Smart"

87) Bill Dana

88) Richard Dawson

89) "Family Feud"

90) Colonel Klink

91) Joan Davis (Jim Backus was the husband)

92) Maynard G. Krebbs (Bob Denver)

93) Grocer

94) Tuesday Weld

95) Zelda Gilroy was the plain-looking girl pursuing Dobie. Chatsworth Osborne, Jr. was the snobbish rich kid

96) Lloyd Bridges

97) Eve Arden

98) Gale Gordon

99) Richard Crenna

100) Gale Storm

101) Mr. Honeywell

102) On board a ship (she was the entertainment director)

103) Phil Silvers

104) Sergeant Bilko

105) Doberman

106) William Frawley

107) Allen Funt

108) Ann Sothern

109) "Texaco Star Theater"

110) Max

111) Danny O' Day

112) Imogene Coca, Carl Reiner, Howard Morris, Sid Caesar, Marguerite Piazza, Billy Williams Quartet, Bambi Linn and Rod Alexander, The Hamilton Trio

113) Jerry Mathers 114) Patty McCormack 115) Wally Cox 116) Tony Randall 117) Jackie Cooper

118) Abbie Dalton

119) Richard Crenna and Walter Brennan

120) Eddie Mayehoff

121) William Bendix (or Jackie Gleason)

122) Peg

123) His son and daughter

124) Neighbor

125) "What a revoltin' development this is!"

126) Ralph Kramden (Gleason), Alice Kramden (Audrey Meadows), Ed Norton (Art Carney), Trixie Norton (Joyce Randolph)

127) June Taylor Dancers

128) Nancy Ames

129) "People are Funny" and "Houseparty"

130) Dagmar, Mama, Papa, Nels, Katrin

131) Clarence Day

132) "Make Room for Daddy"

133) Marjorie Lord

134) Robert Young

135) Bud, Kathy ("Kitten"), Betty

136) Jane Wyatt

137) Springfield

138) George Peabody, Clem Kaddiddlehopper, San Fernando Red, Mean Widdle Kid, Sheriff Deadeye, Freddie the Freeloader, Cauliflower McPugg

139) Spooky Old Alice

140) John Scott Trotter

141) Margaret and Barbara Whiting

142) Elana Verdugo

143) Jim Nabors

144) "Gomer Pyle, USMC"

145) Ken Berry

146) Forrest Tucker

147) Larry Storch

148) Fred Gwynne

149) Ynonne de Carlo

150) Ernest Borgnine

151) Captain Binghampton

152) Dan Rowan and Dick Martin

153) Artie Johnson and Ruth Buzzi

154) "Hee Haw"

155) Caesar Romero (Joker), Burgess Meredith (Penguin), Frank Gorshin and John Astin (Riddler), Julie Newmar and Eartha Kitt (Catwoman)

156) "All in the Family" (Gloria and Meathead)

157) Muldoon and Toody

158) Pat Paulsen

159) "The Jeffersons"

160) "Those Were the Days"

Children's Shows

161) Jon Provost

162) Gramps

163) Jeff and Porky

164) Captain Video

165) "Beany and Cecil"

166) Miss Francis

167) Mary Hartline

168) Buster Crabbe

169) Captain Gallant's sidekick

170) Captain Gallant's son

171) Johnny Weismueller, later played Tarzan in many movies

172) Jim's son

173) Tamba

174) "Ramar of the Jungle"

175) Commando Cody

176) Richard Greene

177) Buffalo Bob

178) Mr. Bluster

179) Clarabell

180) "Nice"

181) Froggy

182) Captain Kangaroo

183) Mr. Greenjeans

184) Bunny Rabbit and Mr. Moose (another "character" was Grandfather Clock)

185) Tom Terrific

186) His enemies were Crabby Appleton and Isotope Feeney, and his wonder dog was Mighty Manfred

187) Heckle and Jeckle

188) Winky Dink

189) Terrytown

190) Oilcan Harry

191) "Kukla, Fran, and Ollie"

192) Micky Dolenz, who later starred with "The Monkees"

193) Jack Sterling

194) "Ho ho, hee hee, my name is Pinky Lee!"

195) David Seville

Miscellaneous

196) Dorothy Collins, Gisele Mackenzie, Snooky Lansen, Russell Arms

197) "The Shrimp Boats Are A-Comin'"

198) King

199) Ajax ("... the foaming cleanser, floats the dirt right down the drain.")

200) David Janssen, the son of Clark Gable

201) Mary Tyler Moore

202) George Reeves

203) Carol Burnett

204) Marian Lorne

205) Durwood Kirby

206) Ross Martin

207) Peter Lawford and Phyllis Kirk

208) Asta

209) Connie Stevens

210) "All aboard for Phillip Morris!"

211) Keith Larsen

212) Martin Milner and George Maharis

213) the little farm girl

214) Ronald Reagan

215) "Toast of the Town"

216) Walter Cronkite

217) Guy Williams

218) Sebastian Cabot, Doug McClure, Joan Fontaine

219) Jack Palance

220) Chick Chandler and John Russell

221) Lloyd Bridges

222) Tagg

223) Edward R. Murrow

224) Betty Furness

225) Molly Bee

226) "Bless your pea-pickin' heart"

227) Ed Ames

228) Dave Garroway

229) Steve Allen

230) Don Knotts, Steve Lawrence and Edie Gorme, Andy Williams, Louis Nye, Tom Poston, Skitch Henderson, Bill Dana, Pat Harrington, Jr., Dayton Allen

231) Jack Paar

232) Pupi Compo

233) Mitch Ayres

234) Julius La Rosa

235) Eddie Fisher

236) "Tammy"

237) "Armstrong Circle Theater"

238) "Search for Tomorrow"

239) Penny Hughes Baker

240) Truman Bradley

241) John Beresford Tipton

242) Michael Anthony

243) Della Street

244) Paul Drake

245) E. G. Marshall

246) Dr. Zorba

247) Dr. Gillespie

248) George C. Scott

249) Reed Hadley

250) Wendell Corey

251) Ben Alexander

252 Craig Stevens and Lola Albright

253) "Mr. and Mrs. North"

254) Tiki

255) Songbird

256) his niece

257) "The Whirlybirds"

258) San Francisco

259) Robert Stack

260) Neville Brand

261) Ben Grauer

262) "Boston Blackie"

263) Herbert Philbrick

264) Efrem Zimbalist, Jr., Roger Smith, Edd Byrnes

265) "Kookie, Kookie, Lend Me Your Comb"

266) Douglas Edwards

267) "See It Now"

268) Bishop Fulton Sheen

269) Dizzy Dean and Pee Wee Reese

270) Victor Jory

271) New York

272) Napolean Solo and Illya Kuryakin

273) Noel Harrison and Stefanie Powers

274) Bill Bixby

275) Charles Bronson

276) Robert Culp and Bill Cosby

277) "Hullabaloo" and "Shindig"

278) Anne Francis

279) Skitch Henderson and Doc Severinson

280) Cleveland Browns and New York Jets

281) Robert Conrad

282) Jack Lord

283) "Cheaper By the Dozen"

284) High School

285) "American Bandstand"

286) nurse

287) Donna Reed of "The Donna Reed Show"

288) "The Wonderful World of Disney"

289) "Marcus Welby, M.D."

290) "Star Trek" (William Shatner and Nichelle Nichols

291) Richard Basehart

292) Bill Mumy

293) Irene Ryan

294) Rod Serling

295) Jo Ann Castle

296) (a) William Shatner (b) Leonard Nemoy (c) James Doohan (d) De Forest Kelley (e) George Takei (f) Walter Koenig

297)   **MATCHING**

Match the t.v. show with the sponsor.

G	1. Wild Bill Hickock	A. Lipton Tea
L	2. Gene Autrey	B. Sealtest
D	3. Lone Ranger	C. Carnation Milk
K	4. Amateur Hour	D. General Mills (Cheerios)
H	5. Jack Benny (later years)	E. Good N Plenty
O	6. You Bet Your Life	F. Prudential
I	7. My Friend Irma	G. Kellogg's Corn Pops
C	8. George Burns & Gracie Allen	H. State Farm Insurance
E	9. Ramar of the Jungle	I. Kool Cigarettes
B	10. Big Top	J. Mogen David Wine
N	11. Your Hit Parade	K. Geritol
F	12. You Are There	L. Doublemint Gum
M	13. Soldiers of Fortune	M. Seven-Up
A	14. Arthur Godfrey's Talent Scouts	N. Quick Home Permanent/ Lucky Strike Cigarettes
J	15. Dollar A Second	O. Desoto

BONUS COMMERCIAL QUOTES

a. Brylcreem

b. Top Brass hair cream. Barbara Feldon (later Agent 99 in "Get Smart")

c. 7-Up

d. Black Label (Carling's Black Label Beer)

e. Timex (John Cameron Swayze)

f. Pabst Blue Ribbon

g. Noxzema Shaving Cream (sexy Scandinavian girl)

h. Gillette Blue Blades

i. Pepsi Cola

j. Anacin (man with headache yells at his wife)

RADIO

298) Paul Whiteman

299) Bertha Brainard

300) Milton Cross

301) Guy Lombardo and the Royal Canadians

302) S. L. Rothafel or Roxy

303) Gertrude Berg

304) Kate Smith

305) Don McNeill

306) Atop the Hotel Allerton in Chicago

307) "Music That Satisfies"

308) Bing Crosby

309) Rosemary Clooney

310) Ruth Etting

311) Eddie Cantor

312) Verne, Lee, and Mary

313) Ben Bernie or Old Maestro

314) "Wanna buy a duck?"

315) clanging gong

316) "Gang Busters"

317) Mary Margaret McBride

318) "One Man's Family"

319) "Information Please"

320) Edward R. Murrow

321) Gabriel Heatter

322) "Your Hit Parade"

323) "Take It or Leave It"

324) Henry Morgan

325) Dunninger

326) "The Lone Ranger"

327) "Inner Sanctum," "Suspense," "Martin Kane," "Private Eye," "Mr. District Attorney," "The Shadow"

328) Alice Faye

329) "First Nighter"

330) "Grand Central Station"

331) "MGM Musical Comedy Theater"

332) "Allen's Alley"

333) Budd

334) "Pepper Young's Family," "Just Plain Bill," "When a Girl Marries," "Marriage for Two," "Rosemary," "Backstage Wife," "Ma Perkins," "Road of Life," "The Right to Happiness," "The Guiding Light," "One Man's Family," "Against the Storm," "Stella Dallas," "Young Widder Brown," "Life Can Be Beautiful," "Our Gal Sunday," "The Woman in My House," "Romance of Helen Trent," "Young Doctor Malone"

335)   **MATCHING**

Match the radio stars to the show or character

I   1. "Perfect Fool"   A. Arthur Lake & Penny Singleton

D   2. "The Fleischman Hour"   B. Jim & Marian Jordan

G   3. "Town Hall Tonight"   C. Ed Gardner

J   4. "Baby Snooks"   D. Rudy Vallee

B   5. "Fibber McGee & Molly"   E. Roy Acuff & Bill Monroe

H   6. "The Aldrich Family"   F. Chet Lauck & Norris Goff

E   7. "Grand Ole Opry"   G. Fred Allen

C   8. "Duffy's Tavern"   H. Ezra Stone

O   9. "Life with Luigi"   I. Ed Wynn

K   10. "Alka Seltzer Time"   J. Fanny Brice

N   11. "Quiz Kids"   K. Herb Shriner

L   12. "Let's Pretend"   L. Nila Mack

F   13. "Lum and Abner"   M. Jan Murray

M   14. "Songs for Sale"   N. Clifton Fadiman

A   15. "Blondie and Dagwood"   O. J. Carrol Naish

COMIC BOOKS

336) Perry White

337) "Great Caesar's ghost!"

338) Sniffles

339) Edgar Rice Burroughs

340) "Brothers of the Spear" (Dan-el, Tavane, Natongo, and Zulena)

341) Smallville

342) Lana Lang

343) Krypton

344) (a) Huey, Duey, and Luey (b) Uncle Scrooge (c) Daisy (d) Gladstone Gander (e) Gyro Gearloose (f) Ludwig Von Drake (g) Grandma Duck

345) Duckburg

346) The Beagle Boys

347) Knothead and Splinter

348) Shezam!"

349) The Flash

350) Tubby

351) Iggy

352) Alvin

353) "Dot"

354) "Little Lotta"

355) Aunt Harriet

356) Dick Grayson

357) "Aquaman"

358) Wimpy

359) Petunia

360) Cicero

361) "Lash Lareau"

362) "Wonder Woman"

363) "The Brave and the Bold"

364) "Fox and Crow"

365) Ollie Owl

366) Black Pete

367) Morty and Ferdie

368) Millie and Melody

369) "Baby Huey"

370) "Hot Stuff"

371) "Li'l Bad Wolf"

372) Don Diego

373) Bernardo, a deaf mute

374) Sergeant Garcia

375) Horace

376) "Chip and Dale"

377) "Joe Palooka"

378) "Turok"

379) "Richie Rich"

380) "Wendy"

381) (a) Mr. Svenson (b) Mr. Weatherbee (c) Mrs. Beazley (d) Betty and Veronica

383) "Little Audrey"

383) Little Beaver

384) Speedy

MOVIES

385) Jon Voigt

386) Sean Connery and Michael Caine

387) Elizabeth Taylor

388) Ricky and David Nelson

389) Elke Somer

390) "The Pink Panther"

391) Steve McQueen was the main character and Karl Malden the villain

392) Alan Arkin

393) Squire Western

394) Molly Seagrim

395) Susanna York

396) David Hemmings

397) Jim Brown

398) (a) Gene Wilder (b) Cleavon Little (c) Madeline Kahn (d) Mel Brooks (e) Harvey Korman (f) Alex Karras

399) Jack Palance

400) Brandon de Wilde

401) Jack Lemmon, Shirley MacLaine, Fred MacMurray

402) United Airlines

403) Marlon Brando, Eva Marie Saint, Karl Malden, Lee J. Cobb, Rod Steiger

404) "Dr. No"

405) Mel Brooks

406) (a) Gene Wilder (b) Peter Boyle (c) Gene Hackman (d) Terri Garr (e) Cloris Leachman (f) Marty Feldman

407) Dean Martin and Jerry Lewis starred and it took place in Cuba

408) disc jockey or radio announcer

409) Stephen Spielberg

410) Jessica Lange

411) Grant Williams

412) Steve Reeves

413) Pat Boone and Shirley Jones

414) Lucille Ball and Desi Arnaz

415) Clint Eastwood, Eli Wallach, Lee Van Cleef

416) Von Helsing

417) Larry Talbot

418) Angela Lansbury

419) Otto Preminger

420) Paul Newman

421) Burt Lancaster

422) Kirk Douglas and Tony Curtis

423) Vincent Price and Boris Karloff

424) Ralph Bellamy and Greer Garson

425) Charlton Heston

426) "Flower Drum Song"

427) Victor Mature and Jean Simmons

428) Phil Harris

429) "Gentleman's Agreement"

430) Bette Davis, Anne Baxter, Gary Merrill, Hugh Marlowe, George
Sanders, Celeste Holm, Marilyn Monroe

431) Gene Kelly and Leslie Caron

432) (a) Marlon Brando (b) Vivien Leigh (c) Kim Hunter (d) Karl Malden

433) Burt Lancaster

434) (a) Steve McQueen (b) Michael Landon (c) James Arness

435) Charlton Heston

436) James Stewart

437) Betty Hutton

438) Frank Sinatra

439) William Holden

440) Peter Graves

441) Ava Gardner

442) Bing Crosby, Grace Kelly, William Holden

443) Betsy Blair

444) Jack Lemmon played Pulver and James Cagney the captain

445) Throwing the captain's plant overboard

446) Audie Murphy

447) Davaid Niven

448) Joanne Woodward in "The Three Faces of Eve"

449) "The Defiant Ones" starred Sidney Portier and Tony Curtis

450) Leslie Caron, Louis Jordan, Maurice Chevalier, Hermione Gingold

451) Deborah Kerr

452) Messala

453) Rod Taylor

454) George Chakiris, Rita Moreno

455) Patricia Neal

456) "Morning Glory," "The Lion in Winter," "Guess Who's Coming to Dinner"

457) Maureen O' Sullivan

458) Sean Thornton

459) Rooster Cogburn

460) Marilyn Monroe

461) "Do Not Forsake Me"

462) Cary Grant, Grace Kelly

463) Marlon Brando was Zapata and Anthony Quinn his brother

464) Kirk Douglas

465) Alec Guiness, William Holden, Jack Hawkins, Sessue Hayakawa

466) Hayley Mills

467) "Butterfield 8"

468) George "Gabby" Hayes

469) Ray Walston

470) Dick Van Dyke and Julie Andrews

471) John McGiver

472) Paul Newman, Jackie Gleason, George C. Scott

473) Jack Hawkins

474) Atticus Finch

475) Jack Lemmon was Felix and Walter Mathau was Oscar

476) Gary Cooper was the star and Karl Malden the villain

477) "One Eyed Jacks"

478) Kim Novak and Rosalind Russell

479) Doris Day and James Cagney

480) Sandy Dennis

481) Glen Ford

482) Rod Steiger

483) Gene Hackman

484) Michael J. Pollard

485) Burt Lancaster

486) Jane Fonda

487) Lee Marvin

488) Nat King Cole and Stubby Kaye

489) Jerry Lewis

490) Leslie Nielson

491) Susan Hayward

492) Jack Nicholson

493) Peter O' Toole played Quixote and James Coco his sidekick

494) Richard Harris

495) Vanessa Redgrave, Robert Goulet

496) Rex Harrison

497) Audrey Hepburn was Liza and Marni Nixon dubbed the singing voice

498) Amazon River

499) Gene Kelly, Donald O' Connor, Debbie Reynolds

500) Anthony Perkins

501) Tab Hunter

502) Sharon Tate (The Charles Manson murders)

503) "From Here to Eternity"

504) Sean Connery

504) Chill Wills was the voice and Donald O' Connor the owner

506) Raymond Burr

507) Glenn Ford, "Rock Around the Clock"

508) Humphrey Bogart

509) Pat Boone and James Mason

510) Raquel Welch

511) "The Day the Earth Stood Still"

512) Cliff Robertson

513) Goldie Hawn and Walter Mathau

514) Judy Holliday

515) "Bob and Carol and Ted and Alice"

516) "Dr. Strangelove"

517) Anthony Quinn

518) Bob Hope

519) Marlon Brando

520) "Day of the Triffids"

521) Ray Milland

522) Frank Sinatra

523) "Love Me Tender"

524) Mary Tyler Moore

525) Roman Polanski

526) Christopher Plummer

527) Robert Mitchum

528) Doris Day and Rock Hudson

529) "Cool Hand Luke"

530) "Lolita"

531) Vincent Price

532) the attack on Pearl Harbor

533) Gordon Scott

534) "Moon River"

535) Bud Abbot and Lou Costello

536) Andy Griffith was the star and Don Knotts the psychologist

537) Michael Caine

538) Sidney Portier

539) Katherine Hepburn, Spencer Tracy, Sidney Portier

540) "Planet of the Apes"

541) Simon and Garfunkel

542) "Plastics."

543) "Butch Cassidy and the Sundance Kid"

544) Ron Howard

545) Kirk Douglas

546) Nautilus

547) Cecil B. DeMille

548) Siam

549) "The Magnificent Seven"

550) "The Man Who Shot Liberty Valance"